DEDICATION

I give all the honour and glory
to my Heavenly Father.
In Him I live and breathe and have my being.

"You are My Inspiration."

I would not have been able to write this book
if it wasn't for the Grace and mercy of God
in whom I was able to endure
innumerable challenges

ACKNOWLEDGEMENTS

Thanks to my family and friends
who believed that I had
a God given gift to write.
I Love you ALL. xXx

Gail Moss USA, The Poetic Evangelist, and
Juliet Ray UK, The Gospel Messenger,
Women of God.
I would not have finished this book
without the wise counsel that
you both imparted.

CONTENTS

CONTENTS

FREE TO BE ME

"He Who The SON Sets FREE is FREE INDEED"

Maureen Morgan

THE CHAOS IS OVER

No more spiritual attacks

No more spiritual disturbances

Thank you Jesus the chaos is OVER

No more spiritual fights

No more sleepless nights

Thank you Jesus the chaos is OVER

No more drama

No more trauma

Thank you Jesus the chaos is OVER

No more heartache

No more pain

Thank you Jesus the chaos is OVER

No more sickness

No more migraine headaches

Thank you Jesus the chaos is OVER

No more hardship

No more lack

Thank you Jesus the chaos is OVER

LOCKED INSIDE MYSELF

I can't move or breathe
The inner pain is driving me insane
I'm so frustrated
I want to demonstrate it
I have so much to give
But I can't seem to live

I have dreams and visions
Why can't I get through this division?
Nothing seems to be happening
My spirit is fighting with my flesh
So much obstacles and challenges
I'm trying to survive

I want to get out of this beehive
And let my spirit come alive
I'm locked inside myself
My spirit needs to be free
I need to come out of this shell
And kick down the gates of hell

I am called for a purpose
I'm not surplus
The real person inside me needs to be free
I asked, seeked and knocked
The doors were opened
Jesus has the key to unlock every door

DEPRESSION

**"Oh my soul why be so gloomy and discouraged.
Trust in God! I shall again praise him for his wondrous help;
He will make me smile again for he is my God."**

I was feeling helpless and hopeless
I lost contact with reality
I lost energy and motivation
I could not deal with simple tasks or decisions

I felt guilty and beat myself up
I felt inadequate, vulnerable and oversensitive
I was going down a dark gloomy road
I was carrying a heavy load

I hated Monday mornings
I did not like to see a new day dawning
I felt sad
I nearly went mad
The Monday morning feeling was bad

I did not want to get up
I did not want to see anyone
I did not want to talk to no one
I had so much anger and resentment
It caused inner torment

I felt like everyone was against me
I carried the world on my shoulders
My inside was in turmoil
I felt anxious, I stopped eating

My hair started to fall out
I stopped looking after myself
I was going through despair
I didn't care about life
I had too much strife
I could not cope
I was losing all hope
Depression affected my health

It disrupted my day to day productivity
Depression reduced my ability to trust God
Excessive worry immobilized me.
"Give all your worries and cares to God for he cares about
what happens to you."

1 Peter 5:7

MIGRAINE

Oh my gosh it's back, the attack
I've suffered with these headaches
From the age of eighteen
I'm in so much pain
It's so intense and immense
Is there no recompense
I feel like I'm losing my sense
Always tense, and in defense
The attack always comes with a vengeance
I keep going into repentance
My life is put on hold
I'm trying to be bold
It debilitates me
Somebody must hate me
My head pounds I hear every sound
The pain seethes through my neck

My back
My shoulders, feel like heavy boulders
I'm sick of being sick
Tired of being tired
Fed up of being fed up
I can't take any more, my body feels sore
I have to be in a dark room
The light makes the pain in my head feel tight
My eyes get blurred, it's obscured

My mouth taste like metal
I feel nauseated I want to puke
But it's the devil I need to rebuke
Get thee behind me satan
THE LORD GOD REBUKES YOU

PAIN

I'm in so much pain and agony
I may look alright to you
But deep down inside
I'm in so much pain and agony
I have a headache and it's not an ordinary one
It's trying to stop my prayers
It's trying to stop me from reading the word
It's trying to destroy me

I'm in so much pain and agony
I have a headache, it's so excruciating
It's torturing and even tormenting me
The pain is so severe,
Lord I'm trying to revere you

I'm in so much pain and agony
I can't sleep, I can't eat, I can't talk, and I can't walk
I can't get around, I feel house bound

This headache is causing a spiritual and physical uproar
I really don't know if I can take any more
I'm in so much pain and agony

My head aches, my neck, my eyes, my back
I have the symptoms of feeling nausea and weak
The doctor diagnosed migraine or stress
I know it's a spiritual ailment
Causing derailment
It's constantly afflicting me

There's no sedative that can ease the pain
It's only Jesus who can deliver me from my affliction
Many are the afflictions of the righteous
But the Lord delivers me out of them all

The pain is so intense from unseen pestilence
Trying to make me loose my sense
This is not vague it's a plague

I shall not die but live
To declare the works of the Lord in my life

Psalms 34:19
Psalms 118:17

FALLING FROM GRACE

I have fallen short of the Glory of God
And although He knew I would fall
God stood tall, even when I stalled
He patiently waited for my call

But I kept falling deeper and deeper in sin
I felt so much disgrace,
I didn't want to seek God's face
God's grace has been sufficient for me

I was experiencing a spiritual fight
Trying to stop me from having a
Personal relationship with God
I desperately wanted to submit myself fully to God
And get into the place where I embraced his grace
I wanted to devote my time to him
And dwell in his presence
Where there is fullness of joy

But because of my sin the condemnation did begin
The devil was telling me that God would
Not allow me into his throne room

God said,
"Come boldly into the throne of grace.
I cried out, Lord I need you in my life today."

I know I have fallen short of your glory
I have done something's that I shouldn't
I was falling so far behind the cross, I felt like dross

Please help me not to backslide
I don't want to hide behind my folly and my pride
Please forgive me Lord and cleanse me
From all unrighteousness
Help me your Royal Highness
Simply because of your kindness

I desire to dwell in the place of grace
Where one day I will see your face
God was able to keep me from falling
There is therefore NOW NO CONDEMNATION
To them which are in Christ Jesus
Who walk not after the flesh but after the spirit

All have sinned and fall short of the glory of God.
Romans 3:23

BROKEN

My SACRIFICE to GOD was an ACT of
OFFERING my HEART and LIFE
My HEART was BROKEN in pieces like a jigsaw puzzle
That I could not put together
I had low self-esteem, lack of confidence

I did not love myself
I failed in every area of my life

My heart was full of anger, hate, resentment
And unforgiveness
It felt so heavy, it weighed me down
The pain inside was tearing me apart

I desperately wanted to make a new start
I asked myself time and time again
How can I be liberated from this deep
Emotional inner pain?

I fell down on my knees and cried out
God create in me a clean heart and
Renew a right spirit within me

I bawled and shed so many tears
My remorse was hoarse, it went off course
I was wailing, shouting crying out loud
I was not proud
I repented in spirit and in truth
I felt a release in my heart
I knew that something did depart
My heart felt empty the pain had gone

A broken spirit and a contrite heart God will not despise
Jesus wiped away my tears and he calmed my fears
He took away my pain and removed my guilty stain

He washed me in his blood
I am delivered and set free
I received the peace of God

Psalms 51:17

UNFORGIVENESS

When I accepted Jesus Christ in my heart
I held onto inner pain, it secretly remained

I was emotionally hurt, that turned into hate
The hurt was buried so deep I could not sleep
It hindered my blessings, and my destiny

God could not work on my behalf until
I allowed him to create in me a clean heart
I had to seriously repent of things known and unknown
And get rid of all the bitterness from the past
And allow God in, to remove the sin from deep within
unforgiveness was one of the reasons why
I couldn't move on

"Do not go to bed with anger in your heart."
That's why my unforgiveness refused to depart
My past was hurtful, people were so spiteful
They despitefully used and abused me
I could not forget the former things
I dwelt on the past
My unforgiveness continued to last

My heart was hard like stone I felt so alone
It made me aggressive and angry towards people
Who genuinely showed me love

I asked the Holy Spirit to bring back to my remembrance
All the people who I held onto in my heart
I called their names and sent them
Love and peace in Jesus Name
I prayed and asked God to save my enemies
I said, Father forgive them for they
Don't know what they have done
I honestly thought I had forgiven them
How can I forgive, and don't forget
What they did to me

The awful memories were still lodged in my mind
If God can forgive me and put my
Sins in the sea of forgetfulness
I made peace in my heart with my enemies
And have the LOVE OF GOD for them
I REPENTED before God with a SINCERE HEART
To receive total HEALING and RESTORATION

Matthew 5: 43-45

THE CRUSHING

I'm just a lump of clay being grounded, pounded and
rounded
My whole body is going through a process
Put into shape by the potter
Who makes the fire get hotter
Gathering the fragments of all the broken pieces
Everything in my life that fell apart
My dreams, vision, and destiny

God has chosen me and he wants to use me
He will not lose me and allow the enemy to bruise me
I have to go through the crushing and the brushing
Before I'm polished and shined
All the impurities are crushed right out of me
I feel like I'm in the grinding mill
The Lord won't let anything spill because he loves me still

I grumble but eventually I have to stay humble
I'm so scrunched up
Like a bunch of olives being trampled on
By people who have walked all over me
And put me down just trying to steal my crown

I was crushed in my spirit, my mind and my body
I felt hard pressed on every side
The four walls closing in on me
At home, work, 'around family and friends' and in church

A lot of people can see that my head is anointed,
So they've become disappointed

They discuss my hair, my clothes
And they cuss and fuss and kick up a rumpus
They can see that the anointing is rich
And my enemies want to see me fall into a ditch

They want to stop me from fulfilling the call on my life
They throw arrows through their words
And darts to my heart
They cut their eyes and they tell lies
I have to go through the crushing
For the glory of the Lord is upon me
I go through the washing of the blood to
Be a clean vessel for the Lord
The lord made me go through the crushing
All the things that was not good for me
The Lord crushed into sand
And now my name is written in the palm of his hand
His glory shall be revealed
THROUGH THE CRUSHING

GOD'S GRACE

My God is gracious and merciful
Many times I turned my back on him
He has never left me, nor forsaken me
I felt like nothing, but God said, I'm something
I wanted to give up, but God said, "NO, YOU CAN DO IT"
I did things that he disapproved of, but God was
Always waiting to correct and comfort me
I said things that I should not, but God forgave me
I thought about things that did not edify my mind,
Spirit, or my soul.
But God was always there to make me whole

My life has been a mixture of good and bad experiences
So much different circumstances
And spiritual disturbances
I'm always doing things that God does not approve of
I sin in word, thought, and deed,
And God is truly a friend indeed
I tried so many things and left God out
And walked through the wilderness filled with distress
I went through the fire and the flood,
Without his precious blood
I went through the storms of life,
But God always took away my trouble and strife
I have Eternal Life
I nearly died but God graciously saved me from death,
When it stared me in the face.

I will continue this race, and dwell in the secret place
I will win this spiritual fight with all my might and
Put that devil to flight
My God is so patient, loving, and kind
I will never find a Father so dear to my heart
His Grace and Mercy has brought me through the drought
I know without a doubt that I will sing and shout
I will bless the Lord at all times
His praise shall continually be in my mouth
BLESS THE LORD OH MY SOUL AND ALL THAT IS WITHIN ME

Psalms 103:1

I DON'T LOVE ME

A lot of women are insecure about themselves
And we're so good at hiding how we feel
We lack confidence, self esteem and the ability to love
ourselves
God created you and I
He loves US
We should love OURSELVES.

I DON'T LOVE ME
I hate ME
I dislike so many things about ME
I'm my worst enemy ME
There's no beautiful features in ME
I have issues with ME
I have so many LABELS that I have placed on ME
I'm not happy with ME

My stomach is too big
I have love handles
I have Michelin tyres around my waist
WHERE'S MY WAISTLINE
My nose is too big. My nose is too small
My lips are too big. My lips are too small
I FEEL SO UGLY
I WANT A PERFECT FACE
I find everything is wrong with my face
My face is too round. My face is too narrow
My face is too small. My face is too long
I SHOULD BE HAPPY WITH ME

My skin tone is too dark. My skin tone is too light
My skin tone is too pale
I have blackheads. I have spots. I have pimples
I'D PREFER DIMPLES
My bum is too big
My bum is too small
My bum is too flat
I've got bags under my eyes
I have dark circles around my eyes
I have chubby cheeks
I WANT CHEEKBONES

I DON'T LOVE ME
My teeth are not white
My teeth have gaps
I wear braces
I WANT MY TEETH WHITENED AND STRAIGHTENED
My hair is too short. My hair is too curly
My hair is too thick. My hair is too thin
I WANT STRAIGHT LONG HAIR
I'M ALWAYS COMPLAINING ABOUT SOMETHING
GOD CREATED US
HE LOVES YOU
YOU SHOULD LOVE YOURSELF
My hips are too wide
My hips are too small
My legs are too long
My legs are too short
My legs are like tree trunks
I have bandy legs
I have bow legs
My legs are stumpy
I FEEL SO FRUMPY

I'm too short. I'm too tall
I have thunder thighs…
WHHHHHHYYYYYYY
My back is too long
My back is too wide
I WANT TO RUN AWAY AND HIDE
I don't have nails. My nails are too brittle
I keep biting my nails
WHY ARE MY NAILS SO FRAIL
I'm too fat
MY DIET IS SEEFOOD… I SEE IT AND EAT IT
These diet pills are making me ill
I HATE WHAT I SEE WHEN I LOOK IN THE MIRROR
I WANT TO LOOK THINNER
ALL MY CLOTHES FEEL TIGHT
I DON'T WANT CELLULITE

I DON'T LIKE MY PEAR SHAPE
I DON'T LIKE MY APPLE SHAPE
WHY DOES THE WORLD COMPARE MY SHAPE TO A FRUIT
EVE ATE THE FRUIT FROM THE GARDEN OF EDEN
IS THAT THE REASON WHY WE
STRUGGLE WITH OUR IMAGE?
I WANT TO BE A COCOA COLA BOTTLE,
WITH CURVES IN THE RIGHT PLACES
YOU KNOW WHAT I MEAN, EVERYTHING INTERTWINES
YOU LOOK SCULPTURED AND FINE,
AND YOU WALK IN A STRAIGHT LINE

I DON'T LOVE ME

GOD CREATED YOU
GOD LOVES YOU

YOU ARE WONDERFULLY MADE
YOU ARE BEAUTIFUL
THE REAL YOU IS INSIDE YOU
BEAUTY IS FROM WITHIN
AND IT RADIATES OUTWARDLY
DON'T WORRY ABOUT WHAT YOU CAN'T CHANGE
ACCEPT WHO YOU ARE
ADMIRE YOU
APPRECIATE YOU
BE HAPPY WITH YOU
BE PROUD OF YOU
JUST BE YOU
CELEBRATE YOU
DESIRE TO BE YOU
LEARN TO LOVE YOU
LOVE YOUR LUMPS AND BUMPS
LOVE BEING YOU
THANK GOD FOR YOU
WORK WITH YOU
YOU ARE UNIQUE
YOU ARE UNUSUAL
YOU ARE SPECIAL
LOVE YOU

SCARED OF LOVE

Why does love hurt so much
Why won't I allow God's perfect love
into my heart and cast out my fear
I am scared of being hurt all over again
The fear of being loved is stopping me from moving on

Why does love hurt so much
Why does the pain still remain
No one really understands why I refuse to say, "I love you"
I find it so hard to say such a powerful word
How can it pass my lips
When my heart has been ripped
I'm scared of love
The love I know hurts
What is love
Will I ever love someone
Will a man truly love me
Will I ever be able to receive his love

Everytime I take a breath
I physically feel the pain pulling on my heart strings
Is there unforgiveness, resentment, and bitterness
The pain seems to be so deep
It makes me want to weep and weep and weep
It's so unbearable and seems unrepairable

My heart feels like a knife embedded deep within
It's digging, poking, even choking
I need to be released from my inner pain
And start to love again

I must believe that God will mend my broken heart
And allow his love to flow through my veins
And pump new life and take out the strife
Perfect love casteth out fear
GOD IS LOVE

EVERY WOMAN

Let us celebrate and appreciate the women in our lives, our mothers, sisters, aunties, friends, and cousins. As women we are creatures with beautiful features. We are fearfully and wonderfully made, God's handmaids.

Let's reflect on all our accomplishments, our achievements, our successes, our failures. Let's remember the good and the bad, the happy and the sad times.

We are independent, wise, responsible, reliable, and knowledgeable and qualified to do any job. We are truly capable and able

Many of us have been through a lot, and the truth about our personal experiences has never really been told, but we walk around as vessels filled with pure gold.

A good number of us have gone through traumatic disturbances that we don't understand. We ask ourselves this question, "Why me?" Why not you? Just like Job your faith has to be tested and tried by God. Our problems did not break us; it made us stronger, with the determination to hold on longer. We have grown over the years through many fears and tears. Ladies we've matured through the tests of time and we're still here to testify about the goodness of Jesus. We've made it, simply because of God's grace and mercy.

I'M EVERY WOMAN the setting stone in my family

I'M EVERY WOMAN I cry and sigh but I still get by, when I lift my head up to the sky

I'M EVERY WOMAN when the bills are high and the funds are low, you would never know

I'M EVERY WOMAN a tower of strength

I'M EVERY WOMAN powerful in my own right.
I will stand and fight the good fight

I'M EVERY WOMAN I have inner strength

I'M EVERY WOMAN caring and always sharing

I'M EVERY WOMAN a shoulder to cry on

I'M EVERY WOMAN affectionate and considerate

I'M EVERY WOMAN with ambition not competition

I'M EVERY WOMAN with hidden treasures beyond measure

I'M EVERY WOMAN I have creativity and versatility

I'M EVERY WOMAN I can do anything when asked
I am multitasked

I'M EVERY WOMAN whose child, is in the mental institution
GOD WILL BRING RESTITUTION

I'M EVERY WOMAN whose child is on drugs
GOD WILL DELIVER AND SET FREE

I'M EVERY WOMAN whose child is in prison
GOD WILL BRING REMISSION

I'M EVERY WOMAN whose child lost their life
through guns or knife
GOD WILL TAKE AWAY THE STRIFE

I'M EVERY WOMAN going through bereavement
GOD WILL GIVE YOU PEACE

I'M EVERY WOMAN who tells everyone the wedding is off
GOD HAS KEPT YOUR TEARS IN A BOTTLE

I'M EVERY WOMAN whose been through shame and taken
the blame
GOD WILL TAKE AWAY THE EMBARRASSMENT

I'M EVERY WOMAN whose life has gone off course because
of divorce
GOD WILL RESTORE YOU

I'M EVERY WOMAN who prays for another woman's healing
and strength from a broken relationship
GOD WILL BUILD UP

I'M EVERY WOMAN who has another woman's back I don't
launch a jealous attack
GOD WILL PROTECT

I'M EVERY WOMAN who does not take another woman's
man. The way you get him, is the same way you'll lose him
GOD SHOULD CHOOSE HIM

I'M EVERY WOMAN who thinks about another woman's
feelings
I'm not into man stealing
GOD WILL BRING HEALING

I'M EVERY WOMAN who committed fornication and
adultery
GOD WANTS YOU TO RESIST SIN

I'M EVERY WOMAN whose been through abortion
GOD WILL TAKE THE CONDEMNATION

I'M EVERY WOMAN who got pregnant out of wedlock
GOD WILL LOOK AFTER THE FATHERLESS CHILD

I'M EVERY WOMAN a victim of rape.
There is no more red tape
GOD WILL COMFORT THE DISTRESSED

I'M EVERY WOMAN going through domestic violence
I will not stay silenced
GOD HEARS THE CRY OF THE AFFLICTED

I'M EVERY WOMAN who's been deceived by a man
but still believes
GOD IS NOT A MAN THAT HE SHOULD LIE

I'M EVERY WOMAN the missing rib to that special man
GOD HAS A PLAN

I'M EVERY WOMAN who tarried and got married
GOD FULFILS HIS PROMISES

I'M EVERY WOMAN who put up with lies and false
accusation
GOD WILL TAKE AWAY THE FRUSTRATION

I'M EVERY WOMAN who gives compliments not judgements
GOD IS JUDGE OVER ALL

I'M EVERY WOMAN whose faith is weak
GOD IS MADE STRONG IN YOUR WEAKNESS

I'M EVERY WOMAN going through the storms of life
GOD WILL BRING CALM

I'M EVERY WOMAN going through rejection
GOD WILL BRING PERFECTION

I'M EVERY WOMAN walking around with years of
unforgiveness
LET IT GO...GOD FORGAVE YOU

I'M EVERY WOMAN through heartache and pain
GOD SENDS SHOWERS OF BLESSINGS IN THE RAIN

I'M EVERY WOMAN when disappointed
GOD HAS ANOINTED

I'M EVERY WOMAN when I feel used and abused and even
confused
GOD IS NOT A GOD OF CONFUSION

I'M EVERY WOMAN when I could not cope
GOD GAVE ME HOPE

I'M EVERY WOMAN valuable and incomparable

I'M EVERY WOMAN a praying mother, wife, sister, cousin
and friend

I'M EVERY WOMAN virtuous and absolutely fabulous

I'M EVERY WOMAN I am called LOVE

I'M EVERY WOMAN young, fresh and green a beautiful
QUEEN

WOMAN OF GOD

Your father loves you so much
You are precious in his sight
You are written in the palm of his hands

For he knows the plans he has for you
They are for good and not evil
Fear not God is in control of your life

Faith is the key to open the doors
Just hold on, and trust him
There is a set time for everything

Woman of God Stand still and see
the salvation of the Lord
He will do what he said, "He will do"
Keep looking to the hills from
whence cometh your help

Nothing is too difficult for God
Continue to pray
Seek his face
Wait for the answers
God will come through for you

Woman of God walk in righteousness and respect
God's values and principles
Uphold your integrity

Be patient and wait
Serve God with diligence
Be still and know that he is God
Be thou HOLY for God is HOLY

Woman of God STEP OUT IN FAITH

LOVE LETTER

MY BELOVED
I openly confess my love for you.
I want the world to know, how much I love you.
I want to shout it from the roof tops,
Until my voice touches the skies and I get butterflies.

When I look towards Heaven
I hold my breath and count to seven.
You take my breath away.

My stomach ties up in knots
When you sweetly call my name.
You remain the same.
You never make me feel blue.
It's all about YOU.
You created love, for you are love.

I am able to love you
Because you taught me how to love YOU.
You're deep in my heart, that's where I start.
Our love is relational and your love for me is unconditional.
I was born to feel affection for you.
I adore you.
I worship you.
I am totally devoted to you.
You first loved me, even when I didn't deserve it.
When my heart was far from you,
You still pursued and wooed me.
You shaped my heart.
How can I depart?

Your love has no limits.
You tenderly protect me.
You never reject me.

You love me with an everlasting love.
There is no beginning or end.
Your love truly transcends.
Our relationship is personal not controversial.
The closer I get to you, the more I know you.
Your love is REAL.

When I'm sad you hug me.
You wrap me in your arms.
I fear no evil.
When I need guidance you hold my hand and lead me.
When I am weary you carry me.
When I cry you wipe away my tears.
Every tear drop is kept in your bottle, you have not
forgotten.

Your word is your bond.
I am fond of you.
You keep your promise.
When you glance into my eyes I'm lost in you.

Your LOVE makes me feel complete;
you sweep me off my feet.
When I'm in your presence there's a sweet essence.
You ease my mind when I feel frantic,
you speak so romantic.
Your words are soft like oil,
and soothe me when I go through turmoil.

I don't want our relationship to cease.
There's so much peace.
I love you because you FIRST loved me.
I love you because you never leave me nor forsake me.
I love you because you are my source of strength.
I love you because you are my comforter.
I love you because you are my redeemer.
I love you because of your warm embrace and the touch
of your face.

I love and respect your grace and mercy.
You always forgive me.
My heart is filled with so much love for you.
I love the beauty of your holiness;
I love the splendour of your glory.
I love the awesomeness of your Royal Highness.
I admire you and hold you in high esteem.
You are supreme.
My King I love when you sing.
My sweetheart I've fallen for you.
My darling there's none like you.
I meet you in the Secret Place
where I dance and delight myself in you.

I love 'Our secret Rendezvous'.
I feel free to talk to you.
I hear your still small voice whisper in my ear.
You tell me how much you care.
I love the special times we share.
I am in awe of you.
I appreciate YOU.
Your love humbles me
I kneel down before you
and bow in reverence.
Your LOVE is the GREATEST GIFT

GOD YOU ARE THE ULTIMATE LOVER OF MY SOUL

YOU ARE MY ONE & ONLY TRUE LOVE

I LOVE YOU xXx

TRUE WORSHIP

It's not where we worship that counts,
But how we worship
Is your worship spiritual and real?
Do you have the Holy Spirit's help?
For God is spirit, and we must have his
Help to worship him in spirit and in truth
Worship is a form of expressing your love to God

It's an intimate relationship that you have to build daily
It's the wellsprings of life that flows from your heart
It's like rivers of living water flowing out of
The depths of your belly
Its prophetic worship when you sing in the spirit
With utterances from God
It's singing songs straight from
Gods throne room of Grace
It's being connected with the angels of God
It's getting the lyrics for songs and poems from heaven

It's getting lost in the presence of God
For in the presence of the Lord there is fullness of joy
You feel so much peace and love from up above

True Worship
It's allowing the spirit of God to be in control at all times
You cannot worship the Lord
If you don't know him personally
You cannot worship the Lord
If you don't allow him to have his way
You cannot worship the Lord
If the Holy Spirit is not leading you

You cannot worship the Lord when your heart is not pure
You cannot worship the Lord when your hands
Are not clean
You cannot worship the Lord in your own strength
You cannot worship the Lord in your flesh
You cannot worship the Lord if you don't relax
You have to decrease so that God increases in you
You have to deny yourself and let God direct you
You have to submit your mind, heart, body, soul and spirit

True Worship
I worship you Almighty God
I honor you
I reverence you
I magnify you
I adore you
I love you
True Worship
Let go and let God

John 4:24

THE NIGHT

The night me and my father danced
was a night I'll never forget

I was in my bedroom...I put on some music
and I started to worship
I bowed down and lifted my hands up to heaven
I started to sing the song to him

I began to feel his presence,
and it smelt like a sweet essence
I fell on my knees asking him to please
help me stay in the inner courts
The doors to the inner courts had opened,
and as I slowly walked into the royal chambers,
like a queen going to see her king

I heard the music change to instrumental
The atmosphere had also changed;
it was awesome, awesome, really awesome
Within seconds I was totally lost in his Holy sanctuary
I heard the sound of strings, and the keyboard rising
through the floorboards
I felt like I was in heaven...I wanted to count to seven,
everything was perfect

I bowed down in adoration without any hesitation
My father pointed his golden scepter towards me, telling
me to come forwards
He then touched me with it,
and as he stretched out his right hand
I stretched out my right hand.
As we touched I felt like I was being
Connected to the main source of my life
So much static and electrical currents running
through my whole body

34

My father gently held onto my hand
The music sounded like a heavenly band
I began dancing and prancing
I could hear the drums beat like the sound of his feet
I felt his heart beat, so I swiftly moved my feet trying not to
retreat from the intense heat

It was like liquid fire taking me higher and
Higher and higher
Oh, the glory of his presence,
Father I give you all the reverence
His hand moved me gently back and forth
I didn't want to let go...I just wanted keep
swaying to and fro

He twirled and swirled me around
My feet felt like they were not touching the ground
I was dancing with my father
It was like the proud father dancing with his daughter
Or, the bridegroom romancing the bride,
who got married because she tarried

The room was filled with such an aroma
I felt like I was falling into a coma
I wanted to drift away and stay with my father
I danced and danced until I became tired

The dance came to an end, and my father did ascend
He went back to the heavenly realms. His dwelling place,
Where one day I will see him face to face
I was quite fortunate to experience dancing here on earth
with my Heavenly Father who loves his daughter dearly

THE NIGHT ME AND MY FATHER DANCED

REAL

Why aren't you being real especially
when we live in the real world

Why don't you face up to reality and confront your
carnality
You say you're a real friend to me,
But you're not being honest with me
I would appreciate the truth from you
Tell me how you dealt with your bad experiences
As a Christian

Why aren't you being real
Please help me understand how I should deal
With real issues of life
Don't just tell me to pray about it,
And everything will go away
Or, be encouraged especially when
I'm feeling so discouraged
Don't you have anything else to say to me
I'm fighting with myself
I need help to be delivered from myself

Why aren't you being real
You say you love me, and you're there for me
I only see you on Sunday
If I can open up my heart to you
And tell you about my past experiences
My struggles and my pain
Why can't you, tell me about yours
Why do you hold back from talking to me
Am I not trustworthy?

We should be real with one another
Give testimonies that are factual
To help someone else
Come out of their mess
We need to be transparent
Pray for each other and speak the truth in love
If we confess our sins one to another
God is faithful and just to forgive
Why aren't you being real?

JEALOUS

Why are you jealous
Shouldn't you be zealous

JEALOUSY IS HYPOCRISY

Why are you envious
Shouldn't you be gracious

JEALOUS NOT ME

Why are you covetous
Shouldn't you be precious

JEALOUS NO WAY

Why are you resentful
Shouldn't you be prayerful

JEALOUS COULD NOT BE

Why are you green-eyed
Shouldn't you be clear-eyed

JEALOUS WHO ME

Whatsoever things are true, honest, just, pure, lovely and of a good report, If there be any virtue or any praise think on these things.

Why am I Here?

I was born to LIVE

But I live to DIE

I can't let life pass me by

Why am I here

I am here to worship the creator

I was created just for that...

I am here in the flesh, but the real me is spirit

I am here in a shell bodysuit

That's why the devil is in pursuit

I am God's temple, a house for God's spirit

GOD IS A SPIRIT

I am here to worship God in spirit and in truth

Why am I here

Am I here to reach out to people?

Am I here to win souls?

Am I here to pray for others?

Am I here to be a witness for Jesus?

Jesus came to serve not to be served

I AM HERE TO... SERVE

Mark 10:45

YOU SEE ME OR YOU DON'T

I notice that you only see me when I look plain and ordinary
But you don't see me when I look extra-ordinary
I never knew that my parents were glassmakers
Am I so transparent to why sometimes
YOU SEE ME OR YOU DON'T

I greet you with a smile and you stare right through me,
you don't even respond, am I invisible to
why you're so dismissible
YOU SEE ME OR YOU DON'T

When I say hello it's like you don't hear or maybe you just
don't care, so you don't acknowledge me
you just dismissed me
YOU SEE ME OR YOU DON'T

You kiss and hug the person right next to me
You have the cheek of the devil to lean over me
How dare you refuse to say, excuse me
YOU SEE ME OR YOU DON'T

Am I too dressed up for you or maybe my hair is too well
groomed to why you walk past me when I stop to talk,
you just walk away with nothing to say
YOU SEE ME OR YOU DON'T

Shall I come in rags just for you to give me a black bag to
put over my head because I know you would
prefer that instead
YOU SEE ME OR YOU DON'T

Why are you finding it so hard to accept me for who I am?
YOU SEE ME OR YOU DON'T

U, '2' SOMETIMEISH

Sometimes you say hello to me
Sometimes you smile wid me
Sometimes you talk to me
Sometimes you walk pass me
Sometimes you look straight through me

U, '2' SOMETIMEISH

It's not my fault God ah tek me higher
An besides you don't know where God has taken me from
Or, where he's bringing me
You don't even try fi get to know me
Don't get me wrong me naaw beg no friend,
Because fi you bad reaction towards me,
Shows in your action
I have tried talking to you
But you gi me de cold shoulder
And dat just mek me bolder

THE GREATEST COMMANDMENT IS TO, "LOVE"
So how can you claim fi LOVE GOD
And you don't know how fi love me, "U NEIGHBOUR"
Where supposed to love one another like sister & brodder
Too much likkle groupie inna de body of Christ

If God is NO RESPECTER OF PERSONS
Who are you to disrespect me
I might not deh inna de clique, but me no say me unique
The bredren should unite as one
But instead there is discord
Flying fast just like de concord
But guess what, I'm here to stay whether you like me or not
I'm not here to fake it, but to make if for Jesus Christ

U, '2' SOMETIMEISH

SWEEP UNDER THE CARPET

Why are you trying to conceal your problems
By sweeping the mess under the carpet
Are you hoping that it will all go away

It won't disappear, when something else goes wrong
It instantly re-appears
The dust begins to fly around never staying on the ground

The rubbish in your life is beginning to look like a molehill
The dirt is piling up

You try to hide your mess behind your fancy dress
How can your mess become your message?
If you keep sweeping it under the carpet

Don't sweep it away and pray that it will stay
You're only brushing your problems, and secrets, aside
You cannot hide from God

If we spring clean the carpet in our natural homes
Your spiritual house can also be swept clean
Your body is the temple of God
let the Holy Ghost cleanse you
Set thine house in order

REJECTION

REJECTION is when people are hostile towards you
They don't like having you around
They don't like YOU
REJECTION has no OBJECTIONS when ill treating you
You're ignored, and rebuffed
If you try to have a conversation, you receive a negative
response
You sense animosity
You're not accepted, only rejected
I could be your missing link, if you would only stop and think
God did not PICK the CLICKITY CLICK CLIQUE
God does not look for groups
He looks for 'ONE' PERSON and
SEPARATES unto himself
"ONE PERSON CAN MAKE A DIFFERENCE"
REJECTION is not nice, it made me feel, undervalued,
unloved, and unworthy
I was dismissed by many, written off as not being chosen
Mistreated like I was not God's child
People looked down on me
But they will look up to me
People watched my downfall
But I continued to stand tall
Have you ever been rejected
I have...
But guess what
REJECTION gave me DIRECTION
REJECTION pushed me into DESTINY and PURPOSE
REJECTION made GOD FAVOUR ME

Frenemy

Are you my friend or my enemy?

I'm very trusting and value friendship
If you're not for me, you're against me

I need positive friends
I need genuine friends
Friends who want the best for me

Not haters or dictators

Friends who will celebrate me
Friends who believe in me
Friends who will support me in my ministry
Friends, who will pray for me,
Friends who will encourage, and inspire me

I don't need friends who are jealous of my God given gifts
I don't need friends who mean me no good
I don't need friends who are selfish
I don't need friends who will steal my ideas, dreams and
vision
I don't need friends who don't talk to me
I don't need friends who are quick to point the finger
I don't need friends who are not responsible for their own
actions

A frenemy is a secret enemy
A frenemy will love you, and hate you
A frenemy will leave you and forsake you
A Frenemy will stab you from behind

A true friend is close like your family
A faithful friend is hard to find

A covenant friend will agree in prayer with you
An anointed friend will worship God with you

A prayerful friend will empower and invest in you
An inner court friend will surround you with love
An outer court friend you keep at arms length
They're your friend to sap your strength
Can you count your inner circle of friends on one hand?
I have learnt that it's not about the quantity of friends
It's about the quality and sincerity of a friend's heart

ME NAME

Me say every minute dem call me name
Always looking for someone to blame
Dem been talking fi ah very long time
An ah mek me name rhyme

Me nuh see dem
But dem call me name
Me nuh visit dem
But dem call me name

Dem can backbite you see
And me sure dem want fight me
But dem can't touch me

Becar de lord sey he will avenge my enemies
So me leave dem fi gwarn call me name
Dem can't even confront me
All dem can do is watch me

An Criticise me and sey, "She ah no Christian"
Well dem must be ah barbarian
Becar dem can't leave my name alone
Bwoy dem come in, like ah dog a yam bone

Me come to de conclusion that me name mustie great
to why dem ah a create
Me name will be a name dem will never forget

Dem same one ah go run to de shops to buy me
books and CD's
Just fi see, if ah really me
becar dem nuh live by faith, dem live by sight

But dem will still find fault
when dem see de proof, lard what ah reproof
Dem will continue to call me name becar dem feel shame
De lord deh pon my side an none ah dem can be against
me
Leave me name alone

2 Samuel 7:9
1 Kings 8:42

CHAT

You chat too much
An all you do is gossip
You go from house to house
Like you ah house mouse

Why you can't leave people business alone
And mine fi you own
You is ah interfering busybody
Always talking bout somebody

You talk bout dis and dat
Bwoy you really can chat
You need to wear de hat
Call chatty, chat, chat

You blurt out everything
You can't keep nothing in
You really have nuff sin

Buried deep, deep down widin
You not confidential
Bwoy you mouth lethal

You run here, there and everywhere
Acting as a 'TV newscaster
Bwoy you is really a ghetto blaster

Who is your master
God or satan
Well, you should know
Becar you mouth will lead you to disaster

You chat too much
An you mouth ah set everything pon fire
Wait you tongue nuh get tire
You chat too much

James 3:1-18
Proverbs 26 v 22

SWEAR WORDS

"The tongue is a small thing but causes enormous damage"

Swearing is disgusting
Swearing is rude
Swearing is disrespectful
Swearing is undignified
Swearing is foul
Swearing is inappropriate
Swearing is wrong
Swearing is Offensive

Clean and dirty water should not spring up from the same
well
Do you swear?
It could be a bad word or, an oath in the law courts

What does God think about swearing?
Do not swear by heaven or earth
Do not swear by God's name
Do not swear on your son or daughter's life
Do not swear on your own life
Do not swear that God is your witness
Do not say... "I SWEAR TO GOD"

Even in the law courts people hold the bible in their right
hand and say, "I swear by Almighty God that the evidence
I shall give shall be the truth the whole truth and nothing
but the truth"
Some people actually lie and give false evidence in court
Why swear on oath and blatantly commit perjury

GOD IS NOT PLEASED

How dare you use God's name to get out of trouble
Stop using God's name as a curse word
Don't use bad language

Say only what is good and helpful
to those you are talking to
and say what will give them a blessing
You cannot bless and curse with the same lips
Are you a vessel of dishonour or honour?

YOU DETERMINE YOUR DESTINY WITH YOUR SPEECH

Ephesians 4:29
1 Thessalonians 4:7
James 3:5

VAIN GLORY

THOU SHALT NOT TAKE THE NAME OF THE LORD IN VAIN
FOR THE LORD WILL NOT HOLD HIM GUILTLESS
WHO TAKETH HIS NAME IN VAIN
Exodus 20:6-8

The name JESUS CHRIST is being used
far too often out of context,
in vain conversations at work and the media

Do you hear people calling
other religious names in vain NO
The name JESUS CHRIST
is sacred, powerful and meaningful
Be careful with the way
you use the name JESUS CHRIST

Through idle conversations JESUS CHRIST
is not getting the praise,
admiration, or glory that is due to his name.
Do not be deceived God is not mocked

Words often used irreverently

- God's sake
- Christ's sake
- Oh my God
- Jesus Christ
- God Damn it
- Holy Sh*t

Do not blaspheme against the Holy Ghost you will not be
forgiven.

You shall know the truth and the truth shall make you free
Stop using Jesus' name in vain; you will be accountable for
every idle word used whether good or bad.

"But I say unto you, that every idle word that men shall speak they shall give an account thereof in the day of judgement. For by your words you shall be justified, and by your words you shall be condemned."

Matthew 12:31-37
Hosea 4: 6

ADORNED

"You shall not cut yourselves nor put tattoo marks upon
yourselves in connection with funeral rites. I am the LORD"
Leviticus 19:28

You adorn your body with tattoos'
And you say,
"Oh my gosh I love tattoos"
It's so fashionable
More or less everyone's got one
It's the best thing ever
My body looks great
Everyone's doing it
It's the in thing
It's so cool
It's awesome
The colours are so vibrant
I love the detail

Do you follow the crowd?
Are you easily influenced?

Why tattoo a loved ones name on your body
Shouldn't it be in your heart?
Why tattoo a picture of something
or someone on your skin?
God says, "Do not worship idols"

You adorn your body with tattoos'
Some people get a tattoo out of ignorance
Some people get a tattoo knowing, what the spiritual
implications are
Some people get a tattoo because they want to look like
a celebrity

You adorn your body with tattoos'
And you say that nothing is wrong with tattoos.
Tattoos are promoted in a subtle way to fool you
It becomes an addiction that requires God's conviction.

A tattoo is an open door
Unbeknown to you,
your secretly bound in spiritual chains
You've cut your flesh and spilled your blood
Like a human sacrifice
You do it once, twice and thrice
caught in an evil device

"The sacrifice that God requires is
a broken spirit and a contrite heart"

A tattoo is a bad spiritual connection
You need God's HOLY PROTECTION

Oh yes, the tattoo can come off, but that takes time
It cost more to take the tattoo off than to put it on
The tattoo may look invisible once it's off, but you're left
with the scars imbedded in your skin,

You adorned your body with tattoos'
Do you not know that your body is a temple
for the Holy Spirit who is in you,
whom you have received from God
You are not your own; you were bought at a price
Therefore honor God with your body"
This great truth should have a real bearing
on what we do and where we go with our bodies
If our bodies belong to God,
we should make sure we have
His clear "permission"
before we "mark them up" with tattoos or body piercings"

When you know the truth and accept the truth
the truth will make you free. 1 John 8:32

Father God I repent.
Please wash away every ink stain with the blood of Jesus.
Amen

Loneliness

Lord why do I feel so alone
This isolation is causing me so much frustration
I wait in anticipation but I feel so alone
No one tries to understand me
Or, even get to know me as a person

Why am I so lonely?
I'm around so many people, but I feel so alone
No one talks to me,
I'm always ignored, shut out, rejected and not accepted

Being in isolation can be depressing

Why do people detach themselves from me
Lord have you set me apart
God it's breaking my heart

It's not nice to be cut off
I'm feeling so destitute for being in solitude
I feel disassociated
My family disowns me
It really has thrown me
No one cares, or even loves me

My new family is on the streets
I don't have true friends' only acquaintances
People who cause disturbances

A faithful friend who can I find
What a friend I have in JESUS
He's the BEST FRIEND ever

JESUS SPEAKS...

I am your true friend
I will be with you until the end
Isolation is not a bad place to be, you will have the victory
I will bring you out of the drought

I will mold you and make you into a vessel of honour
But you have to go through isolation
How will you know the deep truths about me

Seek me, you shall find me
I will never leave you nor forsake you
Go through your time of isolation and humiliation
I will bring you to the place of exaltation

VIOLENCE & CRIME

"A violent man entices his neighbour,
and leads him into the way that is not good.
But every man is tempted when he is drawn away of his
own lust and enticed."

There is too much street crime just for a measly dime
So much violence and silence
Stabbing and bragging and street lagging
Children disobeying parents,
unruly, and have no respect
for the older generation.
What's happening to our nation?

In our days our parents taught us well
Respect your elders
Don't let me hear that you're fighting on the street
Nowadays, the abusive language and bad attitude
is quite threatening and rude
It's not normal
the demons are working through the paranormal

Today's generation you can't even talk to them
You can't even beat your child
You get reported and sent to court for child abuse

Doesn't the parent have any rights over their child?
God said, "Train up a child in the way he/she should go
and do not hold back from giving them a good spanking
for it will keep them from trouble and hell"

They steal cars, joy ride,
vandalise people's property,
drink alcohol,
have unprotected sex,
and smoke drugs
Gang rape and teenage pregnancies
They hurt and bully other people
No respect for another's property
Steal their phones, money, trainers
So much violence and crime

They use guns and knifes
and take innocent lives
So much perversion
they need the Holy Ghost conversion
We need positive role models
Who is prepared to speak up?
The media is killing our children
Their minds are being filled with corruption
That's causing disruption

Why are we allowing
the youths to hate each other,
commit robberies, burglaries,
theft, and murder
So much violence and crime
the devil is really working overtime
Seeking whom he can devour

*"Obey the government, for God is the one who has put it
there. There is no government anywhere that God has not
placed in power. So those who refuse to obey the laws of
the land are refusing to obey God and punishment will
follow. For the policeman does not frighten people who
are doing right, but those doing wrong"*
Romans 13:1-5

Choose

Life is the breath of God
God breathed into Adams nostrils
and he became a living soul
The breath of God is the air that we
inhale and exhale

Life is being spiritually connected to God.
He is your source of strength
Life is to be alive in the land of the living
Life is to live more abundantly
Life is appreciating who you are,
your family and friends

Life is living right, please don't fight
Life is a precious gift stop the rift
Life is to be cherished and sin abolished
Life is to give thanks to God for seeing another day
Life is to begin with prayer
Life is to give God thanks

And praise for health and strength
Life is a time to rejoice and sing and give glory to the king
Life is to forgive and live in peace
Your life is not in your hands
God knows the time span

Life is to be enjoyed
Life is a journey to heaven
Life is living in love, for God is love
Life should be lived to the fullest,
but in the way that pleases God
When you know who you are
you should shine like a star

We are living on borrowed time
We have limited amount of days on earth
For no one knows the day or the hour when Jesus will return

Will you be ready for the coming of the Lord?
Will you be ready when he calls you home?
Will you be ready when time runs out?
Do not waste your time here
We have been given so many gifts and talents
Do not hide your talents
Do not hide your light under a bushel
Let your light so shine before men so that your
Father in Heaven can be glorified

Use your time wisely
For he who wins souls is wise
We have a work to do for God
We are commissioned to preach the gospel to all the world
There is life after death,
"For God so loved the world that he gave his only son
that who should believe in Jesus should not die
but have everlasting life"
Life cannot dictate what tomorrow will bring
Live today as if it's your last

In death you either go in the grave, or get cremated
There is NO REPENTANCE in the GRAVE
There is a time to live and a time to die
This world is not our home we are only passing through

In death we travel to the land of promise,
or to the land of sorrow
Where you'll wish you had another chance
to see one more tomorrow
To die in Christ is to be absent in the body
but present with the Lord

When the trumpet sounds
the dead in Christ shall rise
and they that remain shall meet him in the air

No one has control over death
The wages of sin is death but the gift of God is eternal life
The soul who sins will surely die.
But the soul who lives right will return to God

JESUS IS THE WAY THE TRUTH AND THE LIFE

At the end of your journey
as a human being here on earth
do you want to hear God say,
"Well done thou good and faithful servant
enter into the Kingdom of God
Or, get thee behind me for I knew you not
enter into hell and damnation

CHOOSE YE THIS DAY WHOM WILL YE SERVE!!!

GOD'S TRUTH

Ecclesiastes Chapter 12 verse 1
Don't let the EXCITEMENT of being YOUNG
cause YOU to FORGET your CREATOR
REMEMBER GOD in the days of your YOUTH
before the days of TROUBLE comes,
when you will no longer
ENJOY the PLEASURES of this WORLD

Do not be DECEIVED by the MATERIALISTIC things
that you SEE
Everything that glitters is not gold

The NAME BRAND and the BLING BLING will not
make you a BETTER PERSON

Do not LOVE the THINGS of this WORLD it's only TEMPORARY

JESUS said I am the LIGHT of the WORLD
YOUTH LEARN GOD'S TRUTH John 8 v 12

Read the BIBLE and get your LIFE RIGHT
WALK in the LIGHT

How does a YOUTH become WISE
The first step is to put your TRUST in GOD

You should have three goals:-

1. WISDOM, to KNOW and DO what is RIGHT
2. COMMON SENSE be SENSIBLE in what you SAY and DO
3. THINK before you ACT

Don't walk in darkness YOUTH LET YOUR LIGHT SHINE

OPERATION WIPEOUT

HELP! HELP!
Someone please HELP!
What's wrong?
I'm not sure the young man is bleeding
It may be another stabbing or shooting
And people are looting

The knife and gun crime is escalating
The devil is obliterating
This is getting really frustrating

Young people stop carrying the knife and seek eternal life
There's no repentance in the grave
Why won't you behave?

Innocent people get caught in your wrongdoings
When a life is suddenly taken, another soul is forsaken
The devil aims to WIPE YOU OUT
Young people be more forgiving
Stop hating and be more accommodating
These are the last days YOU NEED TO PRAY

And God's grace will abound and sin will fall to the ground
The devil is using you to WIPE people OUT
He will turn around and WIPE YOU OUT TOO
The devil comes to kill dreams, steal souls and destroy lives

What's causing these deaths
People argue and fight over DISRESPECT
If you die without Jesus there's no turning back
Everything is dark and pitch black
There is Heaven and Hell
Who will you serve, God or the devil
God is knocking on the door to your heart
Turn your life around and make a new start
NO MORE OPERATION WIPEOUT

GANGSTA

A gangsta's life is filled with trouble and strife
If you're a gang member you're classed as a violent
criminal
Why be in a gang, a group of people who do things
morally wrong together
Can't you be a man and stop acting like the Ku Klux Clan?
A GANGSTA'S LIFE IS NO LIFE

Why are you fighting against your own race?
Don't you see you have the same coloured face?
Race against race it's a shame and disgrace

A gangsta's life leads to prison or the grave
Why pretend to be brave
Do you really want to grow old in prison?
Do you really want to die, and not get the chance to say,
bye
Why waste away your life
TURN AROUND AND PRAY

Stop seeking expensive things
SEEK YE FIRST THE KINGDOM OF GOD
Why live a thugs life
It's really a bugs life
Stop hiding undercover
And start your life all over
A GANGSTA'S LIFE IS NO LIFE

There's too much gang rivalry always fighting against each
other over area codes
This behaviour is crazy mode
North, East, South & West debating whose the best
God will put your folly to rest

Why be a mugger, a robber
Don't you know how to be sober
Some of you are in dis gang ting too deep,
you lose nuff sleep
YOU WANT OUT! CALL UPON THE NAME JESUS CHRIST
AND YOU SHALL BE SAVED
A GANGSTA'S LIFE IS NO LIFE

Who are YOU
You should look at where this gangsta life is taking you
Do you really want to go straight to hell
The broad road leads to destruction
but the narrow road leads to eternal life
What will it profit a man to gain the riches of this world and
lose his soul?

A GANGSTA'S LIFE IS NO LIFE
JESUS IS THE WAY, THE TRUTH AND THE LIFE

DA GUN

WHY DO YOU BRANDISH DA GUN IS IT FOR FUN
BUT YOU'RE ALWAYS ON DA RUN
YOU TAKE SOMEBODY'S LIFE
CAUSE SO MUCH STRIFE
DO YOU KILL FOR THRILL
INNOCENT BLOOD YOU SPILL

You initiate in a gang, randomly take a life with a bang
You'll get a rude awakening for the lives your taking
What goes around comes around, that's a true saying
If you live by the gun, you'll die by the gun
You reap what you sow, don't you know

You're breaking too many hearts
Destroying friends and family relationships
In the name of street ownership

You have BLOOD ON YOUR HANDS
The foolish man said in his heart there is NO GOD
The FEAR OF GOD has vanished from the HEART OF MAN

Why work for the devil
He's using YOU to take death to another level
Let go of your pride in Jesus you confide
It's all about the Holy Trinity and unity in the community

WHY DO YOU BRANDISH DA GUN, IS IT FOR FUN
BUT YOU'RE ALWAYS ON DA RUN
YOU TAKE SOMEBODY'S LIFE
CAUSE SO MUCH STRIFE
DO YOU KILL FOR THRILL
INNOCENT BLOOD YOU SPILL

YOUNG MAN SALVATION IS FREE
HAVE A PERSONAL RELATIONSHIP WITH JESUS
Stop making plans about what you're going to do to your
next victim

GOD HAS A PLAN FOR YOUR LIFE

Why seek, innocence, have you no conscience
You lurk in dark places, hiding your faces
You wear the hood, coz you think you look good

You're feet run swiftly to kill
You laugh and joke about what you've done
You've taken somebody's brother, uncle, or son

YOU'VE COMMITTED MURDER
PUT DOWN DA GUN
YOU HAVE TO GIVE AN ACCOUNT TO GOD
YOU WILL BE JUDGED FOR YOUR ACTIONS
THERE IS A GOD REACTION
REPENT AND TURN FROM YOUR WICKED WAYS
THERE IS HEAVEN AND HELL
PUT DOWN DA GUN
Thou shalt not KILL

Exodus 20:13

I AM BLACK

AND THAT'S A FACT
I'm proud of who I am
But I've been so ignorant
I played with my life and walked right into their hands,
Because I did not understand
I was disobedient to the law of the land
And ignorant to God's laws
My eyes have now been opened
I see these outlaws and flaws

I wanted to learn but no one showed concern
I rebelled and they expelled
I don't have freedom of speech
Whatever I say it's to keep me at bay
I need to PRAY to keep the devil AWAY

From the age of 14 I have not lived my teens
These outlaws have been so keen to see me live unclean
I am now branded a criminal with a record, that's not in
the top ten charts
Why do they keep aiming their fiery darts?

I had a dream that's been
Quashed and squashed
Because the material things I aimed
For, were only white washed
I've been stopped and searched
Thrown in the dirt, I've worn the T-shirt
I've been ridiculed and mocked
Knocked around and blocked,
And shocked by the things they say
I've been intimidated and manipulated

Why am I constantly hated?
For just being created

I AM BLACK AND THAT'S A FACT
Not everyone is bad and to be man handled
It's really, really sad
So much allegations and accusations
Why am I being harassed for being black?

Those who feel it, know it
Lawless people should fear the law
Why do I feel like I'm being held by the devil's claw?

No one should judge a person when you
See them being stopped on the street
You don't know why they're being stopped and the
Majority of the time they don't even know themselves

Yes, some do wrong, some do right, but they still
Have to fight for their human rights
They become offensive and very defensive

Always on the attack and using these words,
"YOU'RE ONLY STOPPING ME COZ I'M BLACK"

There's no more slavery
No more chains
But the mental pain

The emotional torment still remains
I am black yesterday, today and tomorrow,
And because I am black it brings me sorrow

**"Where there is no vision the people perish.
But he that keepeth the law, happy is he."**
Proverbs 29:18

"My people are destroyed for lack of knowledge"
Hosea 4:6

"My skin is black upon me"
Job 30:30

"I am black but comely"
Solomon 1:5

**"Jesus Christ is the same yesterday,
and today and forever"**
Hebrews 13:8

I am a
Black
Leader with
Aspirations
Culture and
Knowledge

I AM BLACK AND THAT'S A FACT

FATHER GOD I WANT TO CHANGE MY LIFE I DON'T WANT TO
BE STEREOTYPED. I REPENT OF MY SINS, PLEASE COME INTO
MY HEART AND HELP ME CHANGE MY LIFE IN JESUS NAME
AMEN

JAIL

Every time I go to court I get a bad report
I committed a crime and now I gotta do the time
I didn't get bail, it looks like I'm going to jail
Jail is a place where some people go off the rail
But in Jesus name I won't fail

I will pray and ask God for forgiveness
Coz being in jail is madness
Father God have mercy on my soul
Protect and guide me and make me whole

Strengthen my mind
Help me to seek you, and to find
Please don't leave me behind
I know you're coming back
I don't want to go off track
Going back and forth to jail

I see inmates get angry, inmates sad
Inmates who act like their really bad
Shouting, fighting trying to survive
It's like being in hell with fear as an overwhelming smell

So much inmates trying to hide behind their thoughts of
suicide
Being in jail is not easy, every day is a struggle
You have no privacy and most of all NO FREEDOM
Prison can break you mentally or emotionally
In jail there's gangs and troublemakers
You get intimidated whilst incarcerated
The bullying is debated and overrated

I wish I could turn back the clock
And stop doing the jail house rock
Take my foolish advice
Do not listen to negative people
Do not be deceived by gang leaders
Do not be brainwashed by gang members
Do not be tempted to do wrong
Do not be influenced at a young age
Do not be lead astray
Do not follow the crowd
Do not believe that if you want something you should,
"Take it." You have to work hard for it.
Do not go down the destructive path,
Broad is the road that leads to destruction

"Stay away from prison"

Mother 2 Mother

We need to sit down and reason about the change of
season
Can you see what's happening in the world today?
Society is making our children lose their identity and
personality to carnality
We're losing our son's and daughters, to street slaughters
Our children are dying, mothers crying and even sighing
No one seems to get to the root of these problems
Your child may not be a victim of gun and knife crime,
but as a mother you should be caring, and sharing
your thoughts and opinions with other mothers

So many mothers are going through silent pain
Their loved one has gone in vain
Where's the encouragement and support
We don't need to hear another bad report
Mother's trying to cope with their loss. It's time to stop
covering it with gloss
We need to make a stand and take hold of each other's
hand
United we stand divided we fall
Mother 2 Mother can't you hear the Heavenly call to
HELP ANOTHER MOTHER

So many mothers feel so alone
What will it take before we take heed
We have the power to lead and succeed
Let us help stop this unnecessary bleed
We need to act now and put our hands to the plough

Mother 2 Mother please wake up
We are living in perilous times
We can make a change before society becomes
deranged
We have women leaders in Government and in the Police
We need to make the bloodshed cease

Mother 2 Mother let us pray and ask God to make a way
for every mother's child

LIFE IS PRECIOUS

"The love of money is a source of all evil. Some have been so eager to have it that they have wandered away from the faith and have broken their hearts with many sorrows"

Life is precious

Why be malicious and covetous

God gives life and takes life

Who gave you the right to take someone's life?

Why begrudge another's possession

One day God will be your judge

Life is precious

Why act so ferocious and atrocious

Can't you be innocuous?

Life is precious

Don't take another's life

1 Timothy 6:10

THE MAN YOU ARE

God knew you when you were in your mother's womb
You are fearfully made
You're specially created, so don't feel deflated
You're not defeated
Don't blame others by the way you've been mistreated
You can be treated with respect
You are a man, who should live by faith in God,
And not by what you see

You are a man who should follow after God's heart
Search your heart and make a new start
The experiences you've had should not make you sad
You're not bad, so rejoice and be glad
You've been knocked down but not knocked out
You should live life without a doubt
You are here for a purpose
You are a man of vision
A man of greatness
A man of wisdom
A man of clear direction
A man of stature
A man of truth
A man of good character
A man of good repute
A man of his word
A man of integrity
A man of honour
A man of valour

You are a man who is the head of his home
A man with order in his life
A man who understands instruction
A man who loves his family
A man of ambition with no inhibitions
The man you are is a MAN OF SUCCESS
Don't you know that you are BLESSED

BELIEVE

I have never seen God
but I BELIEVE in the HOLY BIBLE
People say the Bible has been written by man
I BELIEVE ALL SCRIPTURE IS INSPIRED BY GOD

I was not there when they crucified
my Lord but I BELIEVE that GOD sent his
SON JESUS CHRIST to die on the cross

I never walked and talked with Jesus but
I BELIEVE that JESUS was here 2000 years ago

There is no other name to SAVE me
I BELIEVE that no one can get to the FATHER
Except through JESUS CHRIST. John 14 v 6

I BELIEVE in the HOLY TRINITY
where I get peace and tranquillity

I BELIEVE IN
GOD THE FATHER
JESUS CHRIST HIS SON
& THE HOLY SPIRIT

DO YOU BELIEVE IN GOD
I DO...

John 3:16
Luke 24:1-7
Zechariah 4:6

THE PLAN

Salvation is found in no-one else in all heaven and earth
There is no other name like JESUS
For women and men to call upon to save them
People start to make a stand and take hold
of his precious hand
The devil only discriminates a woman or a man
So don't let him give you another ban

No more captivity, take up your liberty
It's only JESUS who has the plan, so become a JESUS fan
I pray you'll understand that things are getting out of hand
Search your heart, and make a new start
The lottery says, "It could be you"
People can't see their fate that money is making them
hate
Don't let it be too late before you become a live bait

Why win your way to the road of destruction
Especially when the devil only seeks abduction
He comes to steal your joy, kill your dreams
And destroy your life
He's only filled with corruption
What will you profit from gaining the riches of the world
and then lose your soul

Every living soul belongs to GOD THE FATHER as well as the
SON JESUS CHRIST and the soul who sins will surely die
You can lose your soul in an instant
Don't let the love of money keep you
so distant from seeking God
Be more persistent and not so resistant

JESUS PAID THE PRICE, not for a bag of rice
Your soul is priceless, and your days are timeless
Start to think twice who's throwing your dice
Why gamble with death and lose your breath
Your life is at stake, and that devil is a fake
There's too many mistakes please make a clean break,
For your own sake

Take up your cross JESUS he's your BOSS
JESUS CHRIST the man with the SALVATION PLAN
For I know the PLANS I have for YOU

Jeremiah 29:11

JESUS NAME

"Jesus is the SAME
YESTERDAY,
TODAY and
FOREVER"

There is POWER in the name JESUS
JESUS came into the world
and got the BLAME
He died and rose
He took the SHAME
He healed the LAME
Despite his FAME
He remained the SAME

At the name of JESUS
every knee shall bow
and every tongue confess
that JESUS CHRIST IS LORD

Philippians 2:10
Hebrews 13:8

SEEK GOD

Seek ye first the Kingdom of God

Seek God with all your heart, and soul

Seek the Lord whilst he may be found

Seek the Lord before you end up in the ground

It's time to turn your life around.

LOOK for God

SEARCH the SCRIPTURES

until you FIND him...

Matthew 6:33
Matthew 7:7

JESUS SAVES

Jesus saves
When you rave

Jesus saves
When you crave for worldly goods

Jesus saves
When you act brave or misbehave

Jesus saves
When you're on crack cocaine
He takes you out of the devil's domain

Jesus saves
When you're a prostitute
He brings you out of your destitute
And gives you restitute

Jesus saves
When you're an alcoholic
He gives you spiritual tonic

Jesus saves
The lost, for the son of man came to
Seek and save that which was lost

Jesus saves
Even when we were dead in sin
We are saved by grace

Luke 19:10
Ephesians 2:5

REPENTANCE

Dear Lord Jesus

I confess that I am a sinner

Wash me in your blood

Cleanse me from all unrighteousness

I believe that you are the son of God

And that you died and rose.

I repent of my sins

Please come into my heart

I accept you as my

Lord and Saviour

In Jesus Name

AMEN

2 Peter 3:9

BIRDS OF THE AIR

I LOOK THROUGH THE WINDOW AT THE BIRDS IN THE SKY
FLYING HIGH GRACEFULLY GLIDING BY
NOT A CARE IN THE WORLD
FREE TO BE WHO GOD HAS CALLED THEM TO BE...

FREE TO SORE TO THE HIGHEST OF HEIGHTS
FREE TO SEE THE LIGHT OF ALL LIGHTS
FREE TO EXPLORE THE LAND AND SEA
FREE TO BE WHO GOD HAS CALLED THEM TO BE...

GOD FEEDS THE BIRDS OF THE AIR
THEY DO NOT HUNGER, NOR THIRST
WHAT MORE YOU AND I
THERE'S NOTHING TO HINDER THE BIRDS OF THE AIR
NOTHING TO STOP THEM FOR THEY DON'T CARE
FREE TO BE WHO GOD HAS CALLED THEM TO BE...

FREE TO SORE TO THE HIGHEST OF HEIGHTS
FREE TO SEE THE LIGHT OF ALL LIGHTS
FREE TO EXPLORE THE LAND AND SEA
FREE TO BE WHO GOD HAS CALLED THEM TO BE...

HAVE YOU EVER GAZED AT HOW THEY STICK TOGETHER
LIKE GLUE TO LEATHER
THESE BIRDS ARE OF A FEATHER
THEY FLY IN FLOCKS AND CLING TOGETHER
LIKE LOCKS OF HAIR
IF ONE SLIPS BACK THEY SLOW DOWN UNTIL
THE WEAKER ONE CATCHES UP
THEY HOLD EACH OTHER UP
THEY GUIDE AND GLIDE AND KEEP EVERY BIRD AT THEIR SIDE

THEY STAY IN THEIR GROUP A TRIANGLE THAT MOVES LIKE A
VICTORIOUS TROOP

THEY FLY HIGH AND LOW ALWAYS ON THE GO
NO OBSTACLES IN THEIR WAY
NO HINDRANCES
THEY JUST GO WITH THE FLOW
FREE TO BE WHO GOD HAS CALLED THEM TO BE...

FREE TO SORE TO THE HIGHEST OF HEIGHTS
FREE TO SEE THE LIGHT OF ALL LIGHTS
FREE TO EXPLORE THE LAND AND SEA
FREE TO BE WHO GOD HAS CALLED THEM TO BE...

A RAINBOW

I saw a Rainbow in the sky three times in one day
I feel so blessed to be in the land of the living
It was absolutely beautiful to see

On the bus a little boy said,
"Mummy why is there colours in the sky"
His mummy said, "It's a Rainbow"
The little boy asked, "What's a Rainbow"
His mummy replied, "I don't know what it means."

A Rainbow does not mean that you will get "A Pot of
Gold."

A Rainbow signifies God's PROMISE & COVENANT
to his people

God said, "When you see the rainbow, it is a SIGN that
He will never flood the earth like in the days of Noah."
Genesis 9:11-13

The rainbow colours are sevenfold

Red
Orange
Yellow
Green
Blue
Indigo
&
Violet

I CAN SEE A RAINBOW

SPIRITUALLY FIT

"Spend your time and energy in the exercise
of keeping spiritually fit.
Bodily exercise is all right but spiritual exercise is much more
important and is a tonic for all you do"

I was jogging three times a week
I felt the benefits and my body looked tweaked
I feel lighter. I look brighter
I feel stronger, holding on spiritually longer
It's good for the mind
I feel mentally alert
I can cope with any thrown dirt

I have clarity of mind
I am seeking and yes, I do find
I feel great
I love jogging
Never thought I'd say that...
So I'll say it again,
"I love jogging"

I feel like I can run through a troop
Leap over a wall
Jump over hoops
And stand tall
I feel focused
I can see clearly
I know Jesus loves me dearly

Keep yourself in training for a godly life
Physical exercise has some value,
but spiritual exercise is valuable in every way,
it promises life both for the present and for the future

Surely you know that many runners take part in a race,
But only one of them wins the prize

Run then in such a way as to win the prize
Every athlete in training submits to strict discipline,
in order to be crowned with a wreath that will not last
but we do it for one that will last for ever
That is why I run straight for the finishing-line"
I run with PURPOSE in EVERY STEP
I RUN FOR THE PRIZE OF THE HIGH CALLING

1 Timothy 4:7-8 TLB
Romans 5 :3-5
1 Corinthians 9:24-26

THE HEAVENS DECLARE

I wonder do you really know that the heavens declare the glory of God

Day and night they tell about God without a sound or word

The sun lives in the heavens and moves silently across the skies

It shines so radiantly, and nothing can hide from it's heat

The sun shall not smite thee by day nor the moon by night

But it moves across the skies with rays of light

The blue sky sometimes stands still with peace and tranquil

Be still and know that he is God

The angels bow down before God's throne wearing white robes of holiness and righteousness showing their respect

It's truly amazing God's creation

The white clouds are white as snow, so pure they glow

They seem surreal as they move around the sky gracefully

Who can fathom how the clouds change

from white to grey, when rain is on the way

The sun beams O so bright and the angels ascend

and descend in the light,

Answering prayers, and fight the good fight

God's love and grace is awesome

His mercies are new every morning, as we see a new day dawning

God is calling us to arise and inhale the fresh air

You will hear the voice of God it's clear

We see nature at its best, woken from our rest

Thank God for another day

It's so calm just like a healing balm

Seek the Lord whilst he may be found

Don't wait for the trumpet to sound

Every eye shall see him coming in the clouds

Every knee shall bow and every tongue

confess that Jesus Christ is Lord

The earth is the Lords and the fullness thereof

THE SCENERY

A landscape of sun, sea and sky with houses, and trees
It so widespread it's truly amazing
How the earth can be round
But we walk on the ground
It's so strange the way the earth is arranged

So many trees, mountains and fountains,
Rivers and streams rippling down
God spoke the word and the sea obeys and stays
It does not go beyond the set boundaries

The sun shines down on the town
Everything glistens, you begin to listen,
to the sound of nature. Thank God the creator

Everything looks beautiful set in its place made by grace
There is a landmark for everything under the sun
We are not the only one

I thank God that I can go on my knees
And pray for seeing another day
I'm in the land of the living
I need to start giving and forgiving
Not many people are alive
Not many people wake up
Not many people believe in God
But I believe that God created the heavens and the earth
There's no doubt about that, it's a fact
The earth is the Lord's and the fullness thereof
And they that dwell therein

Some people have gone through redundance
But it's a beautiful thing to have life in abundance
There are different shades of green,
Dark green, light green, it's all in between
Oh, it's so serene

The leaves looked scorched
Or, should I say torched when the sun
Dries it out...
Some leaves are yellow,
Some brown when they're ready to fall on the ground
But you don't hear a sound

THE TRUE MEANING OF RELATIONSHIP

In the beginning God created the heaven and the earth and the spirit of God moved upon the face of the waters. God said, "Let there be a firmament in the midst of the waters and let it divide the waters from the waters." Have you ever listened to the sound of the sea? The water is so calming, so refreshing and so reviving. How many of us have stood by the sea and looked at how far and wide God's love is towards us? As far as the eye can see God truly loves you and me. Don't you see what I see. He stretches forth his hand across the sea calling you to come unto ME. Deep calleth unto deep. God wants your relationship to be close with him, and your SHIP will sail across the sea with ease. No one can fathom the greatness and awesomeness of God. You can have a relationship with him and experience his peace and love.

A RELATIONSHIP starts from the time we give our life to God
It is the God ship, forming headship, kinship, cousinship,
Courtship and friendship
It's how we relate and inter-relate to each other like sisters
and brothers. Its being honest, reliable and supportive

A GOOD RELATIONSHIP encourages you, motivates you
and prays with you, but may not always stay with you

SOME RELATIONSHIPS are broken, where too many
bad words were spoken
SOME RELATIONSHIPS have no connections
due to family rejections
SOME RELATIONSHIPS know how to relate and some just
hate
SOME RELATION-SHIP can take you on a journey of self-
discovery
SOME RELATIONSHIPS can bring trouble and strife, as we
travel through the storms of life

SOME SHIPS have gone off course and have divorced
SOME SHIPS have tarried and have stayed married
SOME SHIPS remain single because they just won't mingle
SOME SHIPS have lost their sail but God heard their wail
SOME SHIPS have children, some don't and some won't
SOME SHIPS play truant because they're not fluent
SOME SHIPS are expelled because they rebelled
SOME SHIPS have a bond and some abscond
SOME SHIPS honour and some dishonour their mother
and father
SOME SHIPS trust, some distrust and some just rust
SOME SHIPS join together in fellowship and respect
leadership
SOME SHIPS carried too much junk and they sunk
SOME SHIPS have heavy loads and won't throw it
overboard
SOME SHIPS have a frown and give up on their crown
SOME SHIPS put their anchor down, through test and trials,
but they don't drown
SOME SHIPS move around and around but never
touch dry ground
SOME SHIPS overcome the roaring tide, sail through Jordan
and reach the other side
SOME SHIPS are obedient and receive blessings upon
blessings
SOME SHIPS reach their destination and they possess and
dominate the land

The True Meaning of Relationship is FAITH, HOPE and LOVE
But the greatest of these is LOVE

CHURCH HURT

Why do people in church hurt you
You give and they continue to live off you

You borrowed and they bring you sorrow
You share and they just don't care

You feel so much pain
Why does the hurt still remain
Are you going insane?
No, don't take their guilty stain

They fling so much dirt
It's ruined your shirt, and skirt
Stand strong in the rain
And let the blood of Jesus wash away your pain

Yes, you've tried to be strong
And the pain still prolongs
No one hears your sighs
Only God who sees your cries

You feel so much sadness
It feels like madness
Because of your kindness
You will receive happiness

These people have no shame
And their tongue cannot be tamed
So you're not to blame
For them being spiritually lame
These wolves in sheep clothing can't help loathing

It's not your fault they're so mean
Just keep your heart pure and clean
Show them love from up above
Continue to serve his Royal Highness

God will clothe you in righteousness
Be strong in the Lord and the Power of His might
He will fight your fight,
Jesus Christ. He is the light

Stand and see the salvation of the Lord.

SILENT SERVICE

I serve the lord in silence
When I speak the word of God I am silenced
Someone always talks over me
No one gives me the freedom to speak
I hear them quote scriptures and their words
Just won't cease
I hold my peace

I serve the lord in silence
When I talk in a conversation I don't get to express myself
Or, testify about the goodness of God in my life
Someone else is always speaking over me
I think that's why I'm so quiet
Maybe it's the reason why I write
I don't get the opportunity to speak very much

I serve the lord in silence
Silent rivers run deep and if deep calleth unto deep
All that's inside me will flow out
On paper words just flow, always on the go
I'm free to express myself
I'm free to be me

I will speak the word of God with power and authority
I will speak as an oracle for God

F^RE^E T_O ^BE M_E!

"He who the son sets FREE is FREE INDEED"

Free from ~~condemnation~~

Free from ~~hurt~~

Free from ~~pain~~

Free from ~~unforgiveness~~

Free from ~~stress~~

Free from ~~depression~~

Free from ~~oppression~~

F^RE^E T_O ^BE M_E!

Free as the bee

Free as the tree

Free as the sea

Free to sing

Free to dance

Free to worship

Free to prance

Free to write

Free to be creative

Free to love

Free to travel

Free to express myself

Free to walk in liberty

Free to be happy

Free to laugh

Free to smile

F^RE^E T_O ^BE M_E!

98

GLOSSARY

JAMAICAN PATOIS - TRANSLATION

An	And
Becar	Because
Bout	About
Bwoy	Boy
Dat	That
De	The
Deh	Is
Dis	This
Fi	To
Gwarn	Go on
Gi	Give
Groupie	Group
Inna	Into
Lard	Lord
Likkle	Little
Me	Myself
Mek	Make
Mustie	Must be
Naaw	not
Nuff	a lot
Nuh	Don't
Pon	Upon
Sey	Say
Tek	Take
Wid	With
Widin	Within

ABOUT THE AUTHOR

Maureen Morgan is a mother, author, poet, singer, songwriter, inspirational speaker, strong woman of faith and Evangelist. She endured abuse from a family friend at the age of five. After the death of her father she bottled up her feelings. She was raped at eighteen, and at twenty one a victim of sexual assault at knife point. Traumatized by the tragic experiences, Maureen became reserved and stopped talking, but found an outlet to release her inner pain through writing.